in the middle of things

in the middle of things

WILLIAM KISTLER

PRESS

First Edition: December 2013

studies one, five, thirteen, fourteen, twenty, twenty-two through thirty,
and forty-three have appeared in *The American Poetry Review* with
different title numbers, some of them in slightly different form

Author's website: http://williamkistler.com

iPhone is a registered trademark of Apple Inc.

ISBN 978-0-9890912-1-3
Library of Congress Control Number: 2013947972

Cover design: Carol Haralson
Cover photograph: Michael Collier
Author photograph: Karen Tompkins
Interior design: Douglas Gordon
Composed in Palatino fonts by P. M. Gordon Associates, Inc.

Published by ZIG ZAG PRESS LLC, Philadelphia, Pennsylvania
Distributed by MILLICHAP BOOKS LLC

Available at your local bookstore

Available online:
amazon.com / barnesandnoble.com / iBooks

Available to the trade:
Baker and Taylor: 800-775-1100; fax 800-775-7480
Ingram: 615-793-5000; fax 615-287-5429

or contact MILLICHAP BOOKS LLC
pmillichap@sbcglobal.net

with numberless Thank-yous
to Eileen and to David
and a bow at sunrise to Steve

Why these things knew my name I couldn't say
but I received their call with a kind of innocent joy.

JOEL MEYEROWITZ, photographer, New York

Contents

I

II

III

I

study one

I don't know anything about myself
anymore. I don't know when I may die,
I don't know why. This wrist now is
without pain, I don't know why it hurt.
If I begin to speak I don't know
when I'll stop. I don't know if this insight
will end first, or the words, each perception
drive toward every possibility, or, this
hand assert—*no more words, Good Night,*
I want my dream life's home of sleep.
Trees tell me they die many winter deaths
on their passage back into earth,
while through many summers they gave
passage through rooms of shade. Passage
ended some days or years past when
mornings turned so slowly they felt
like truck wheels backing up a rainy hill,
then round a blind corner, slow,
and then slower still, and so I wake
so late in the night I hear only sand
falling in the darkness of my study
in my grandfather's empty hourglass

study two

not much happened on that day, a day
in which the earth moved some distance
further around the sun, though the sun
appeared to cross our sky and set,
a day in which I waited to write a poem,
no poem opened its eyes and beckoned,
I am still outside, young a little, old,
sad a little, somewhere further on,
until she took me in with her eyes,
yes, I do know, she acts with her eyes,
like a poem with its eyes, smiling,
coming close to my ear, whispering,
pretending to be real

study three

alone in the transparent bag,
not dead but not stirring, as if
they were holding in their own breath,
their flesh now firm between my teeth.
In my father's time I would have gone
with a long stick, beaten them out of the trees,
my thoughts repeating—*strike these limbs*
with a lightness that frees but does not
break them. We recognized each other
from the moment of their first blooms,
took up words with our heads full of almond
fragrance, how can we not speak of them
now, their wrinkled edges continually
fresh against our teeth, their taste
lingering like thought between us

study four

the rice is immediately clean
down to the depth of each grain
grown in the river basin where no
chemical has been, these teeth turn it
into a paste these cells consume.
Her friend crosses in front of her,
I cannot follow her arm where
it begins to enter the sleeve of her coat.
I picture the darkness within the coat,
I picture her arm within it,
I picture the darkness within her dress,
I picture her length. Is it for me
to reach toward the light now dark
in that darkness? is it for her
to imagine it? are we alive
in a room we may never inhabit?

study five

but for eyes accustomed to darkness
colors lie in ambush, light has no age
and remaining alone has no weight,
sometime after I went on a dolphin to visit her
where she was letting the sun's rays
warm her skin, it was morning
on a beach in a twisting island chain
they had randomly named after a youth
who had found the name—Ios—washing
in the sea and taken it for herself,
and, yes, blooms we called flowers
were everywhere about, spreading a sense
of peace and particularly of presence
which later we felt as freedom

study six

the mind electric was the body's
destination, she knelt, looked
into me, her eyes were subtler even
than the passages of her skin, I let
each surround me, the black pupils,
the flame-like strands of the irises.
Did I believe I knew her?
She was a life beyond. Holding
became like knowing without sight,
different, slow-changing tides.
Neither held long to the other
but to a life which angled,
became a plain, a river, light
from which a radiant sun is rising

study seven

see that you may believe, Aquinas may
have said, I see now there were many
things about her that could not be seen.
I might see several in one moment, miss
others spread across a slope of months.
I could see her incisive wit, joined to
kindness, stirred the wind in me, and,
like the turning of a wheel, left a center
of calm between us. She early told me
she did not want the weight of a tomb
or tears at the end, and no flowers from
those who had made war. She saved her
driest irony for mirrors—as in, what
could be more bizarre than continually
reflecting back the continuous changes
of the day, as in, it was not possible she
might believe she could extend the woman
who had the day before looked in, while
month by month she was imperceptibly
losing that earlier woman. I could not
name her full self, or what it was she
hoped she was moving toward. And that
was what I had missed, with the instinct
of a mountain animal, she was as she
was, would always be. *Life has been
lent to us*, she had written to me, and I,
remembering, changed, understood
the continuing of her as the truth of her

study eight

where the pond flowed under the bridge
she stopped the car to turn her head left
toward the beach where it entered the sea,
then right past reeds and fields, houses,
trees, to where it passed under another
bridge and became a stream, this was
a certain place in the middle of things,
as were her eyes looking first one
direction then the other, as was the earth
about midway through its journey
from the eastern morning to the western
evening. Later, searching with a map,
the words of a lost text—*here today,*
then vanishing into what—came back,
as the car rolled onto gravel and the view
revealed a house half-hidden in trees
at the end of an inlet not yet in the sight
line of anyone—calm, with the sound
of water lapping. I thought she might
not mind, *old, somewhat run down,* if
we could see the sun descend as the earth
turned, remember the sense of waking
into time and at the same time falling,
little by little, dissolving, into one,
though holding as two. There we came
to see night, the wash of tides and stars,
as an opening to further light arriving
full from across the reaches of days

study nine

there she was, above blocks of open space,
standing in a roof garden while I was
not quite believing it could be her. We both,
you understand, had overbearing vertigo,
which caused her wave from that height to be
more than surprising, her, with her thick
Irish hair and mid-night impersonations,
myself, with a young man's desire to find
a room in a walk-up top of steep stairs, where,
it happened, I could look out on a small
maple broadening against the sides of its box.
There I was, determined to find a means
to turn the lies engulfing the world onto
their large ends with, *hard to believe*, words
placed on a page. *Hello youth. Hello agonies
of age.* While meanwhile we were middle-
aged and trying to loosen our second fear—
that one of us might change, begin to move
in directions we did not recognize. There,
in the moment of that time, night took up
freedom, legs crossed in dream, sleep entered
sleep, alive we were, in an earlier future

study ten

speak, she then said,
I have nothing I can fully say,
staring into reports, being
paid to speak, being
between being
and having no
knowledge of being
air turns to ash,
ash bears the sun away,
the sea bears houses,
what I have sought no longer exists,
where are you?
I shall not forget you until I wake near you

study eleven

from within a day-long silence
she slowly says, *the two pears*
have spent the day without speaking,
perhaps it's because they have changed in color
and now are dying, yes, and I remember
the oarsmen on the triremes plying the Aegean
did not speak either, nor the soldiers
huddled in the trenches of *the war*
to end all wars, which ended
without ending anything, none
spoke, and we did not demand to hear
what it was they were saying
with their mouths open and no sound there

study twelve

in the name of wisdom give me liberty
for those who pick vegetables so there
can be food, who lie under car-bed-
frames, tighten joints, so there can be
journeys, liberty for those who turn
longing and time signatures into notes,
notes into ink on a page, ink
transcendent into music, where
the beach floats at the edge of the sea
and the sand becomes a window holding
the further shore of sound felt as light—
this day's exact place, it turns out,
for arriving into the transparence of sight

study thirteen

it is clear now that somewhere beyond
four thousand of earth's turnings
and, yes, some considerable
cycles of time before Jesus the Christ,
the scribe took his seat beside the old man's
throne, to record what the new general
now called his own, and who
among his fathers/mothers, sons/daughters,
he had chosen to continue
his house and hierarchical invention,
clear then that the women there
no longer stood beside him,
the word was at the center,
the scribe's marks were on the stone,
the priest's speakings established remembering,
the word was at the center

study fourteen

everything goes into lock,
money freezes in the ether,
people freeze in the air
beneath, no one knows
what to think, each seeks
immediate relief,

insurance, assurance,
citizens to pay cities
cities to pay states
states to pay banks,
banks to hold the book

which now is too large
to open, things dis-
locate, nothing fits,
each must further pay
to own the code to close
what they already own,

interest spun into chains,
every line extended,
production unfinished,
layers of counter, and
counter on top of counter,

obligations, grinding,
rusting, no reduction,
lower, slowing, continual
slowing—bonds, buildings,
abandonment, mountainous
despair of beggar's dust

study fifteen

one look at those crack troops standing
at perfect-to-the-last-button-end attention
and one knew that nothing good could come to
anyone anywhere near that walled compound,
was it Dostoyevsky, was it Montesquieu,
who said, *"power corrupts and absolute*
power corrupts absolutely", they knew
about beatings, starvation, cold, as the
beginning of man's inhumanity to man,
and after the beginning the desire to own
the means of production, the medium
of payment, the methods of employment,
the terms, and after that the desire to own
the institutions of order, and if anything
is left standing the Agency will realign it,
the crack troops will be there with black clubs,
no doctors, philosophers, musicians, blood
won't be seen, bullets will not initially be used

study sixteen

in my waking mind I say this to you
my sometime friend, sometime enemy,
you don't own me if you can't find me
and I don't exist if I can't be heard.
Always the feeling that neither of us
knows the other, that each struggles
as if at the edge of birth to emerge,
even if only partly complete. I
thought I was free—what innocence,
you thought you owned me—what simplicity,
your next direction is almost always
something I know already but cannot
contain, as you cannot contain me,
we must draw back, let the sun
widen the space between, night will be
coming upon us, we will need to see

study seventeen

my eyes leave the writing page,
first light of morning arrives
shaped by fronds of palm, finds
beads of rain from a passing shower,
fills them with light — worlds are born.
I return to measureless, imagined
rooms of mind, for seconds? for minutes?
perhaps for centuries within the gravity
of another time. I lift my sight again,
the sky is close, the clouds, thin,
drawn tight, wrinkled like one of us,
this mind is loosened, floats before itself —
the beads are gone, the clouds rising,
I am near the end of my life,
a man released by fate to live for a time
beyond these days which every day
bring to light our continuous bending
over and taking up of the person-
against-person flames of fire and fear

study eighteen

here is what takes place in front of us—
explosions, rubble of buildings, destruction,
waterworks, gone, plumbing, gone, water
itself, beautiful clothes, work clothes, gone,
furniture to sit on, eat on, food also,
each person's sleep, gone, precious letters,
indispensable records, photographs of those
we knew well, gone, paintings of the garden
from its beginnings, the garden itself, gone,
people and skills, more people and all skills,
crockery, cars, sculpture, gone, every kind
of tree, the social contract between people,
the law surrounding the contract, nothing
saved, centuries of lifting up and fitting
together, gone—*look*, though it seems to be
taking place in a distant place, to a different,
alien other, that darkness invades this air,
stains this swelling sea, loss leads to loss,
nothing saved, people don't return, the years
wash over, none return, craters of sadness,
rubble covered by what the wind brings,
wounded eyes lost in the mind of loss

study nineteen

no matter how hard we tried
bugs got in the bed and water
flowed over the banks of the river
bringing mud, the grass died
and the beam broke in the wind,
this is what we find getting old to be,
though what we have also received
is a general weakening
of the remaining parts of the body
and some loss of hearing,
it's also important to try
to remember the story is not ended,
more is sliding and will fade
before the winding of our own day
goes to the window, looks out
on songs, on whispers, on the other
dream-intimations of memory
arriving from the place
beyond our furthest memory

study twenty

these wounds are small
compared to fighting with those I love,
I had just evaded a shot aimed from above
when the central beam fell burning upon me,
things above are supported by those of us
beneath, I will not speak of the pain,
I will say fate smiled upon me,
I am now beyond,
intention moves alone in these shadows,
I get on a bus
under a sky lonely for the moon,
travel through gates of time which dis-
solve before me, arrive no final place, find
only what I left drenched anew with sun,
one hand later gives a hand to another,
in that exchange two roses
are as good as three

II

study twenty-one

I would return to that room,
it would be silent, holding its beige color
like an open sunset in its open hand,
the minute hand motionless in movement,
she however would be as full
as she was in sleep, her pen sometimes
quick across the page, sometimes silent,
building images which filled the room,
flooded into the frames of pictures,
called to this quiet I, itself receiving
inexhaustible memory where her arched
foot disappeared into her black slipper,
itself disappearing into the shadows
held beneath the legs of the table

study twenty-two

you can't know what anything is like
until you have lived it, I keep remembering,
I thought her brother was calm, steady,
even after his wife told me otherwise,
I, yes, did think I was calm, collected,
until one night when I stood straight up
between two men who had my money,
were reaching for my watch, the one thing
to the side of his wisdom my father
had left me. I swung my right hand,
ran to the avenue, up the center lane,
not looking back, expecting a knife to cut,
flesh to cry out, no, not as collected
as I thought, willing to risk all to have
one moment each day when looking
into this time face, a slow, night voice
might speak, telling me his father
and his father, both, were there with me,
never would leave as long as peace
remained in that place of broad oak
trees, silent macadam streets, midnight
trains loosing their long warnings
before they reached the gateless crossings

study twenty-three

she is moving in the close darkness,
later her rounded form sleeps, slow rolling
inhalations/exhalations from which body
warmth is released, and after an extended
stretch through the cover and blanket of night
rapid eye movements begin to reflect
fitful dreams — lost children, lost lovers,
flooded houses — faster she wakens
through the warp of dark, rolls against
his length, he is listening to the closing
of a door, sensing what does not fit,
a seam in the silence admitting faces,
threat of danger. Where fear of snakes
and flying creatures move in deep,
primal memory, danger now is moving.
This man, this woman, the vigilant
and the sustainer, the defender and the giver
of warmth, share calm and fitful sleep,
the north and south of living history,
the bed of fear and the bed of waking,
the bed of love and the bed of sadness

study twenty-four

out of the remembered cave of the breath,
a deeper breath, from there I see the stag
clear the fence and if there were no bullets
it would seem he would live forever,
your face is at the window, drop by drop
rain is falling from your hair, broadening
where each lands with the weight of white
petals, with a clank the gate closes,
signaling the beginning of an ageless sky,
the falling through of a moment

study twenty-five

almost smaller than this eye can see
ants appear as if from celestial ether,
as if without a line or point of entrance,
from every grouted seam, indeed,
from under the bread toaster, the oven lid,
the dish stacking rack, the knife block,
the rounded base of the coffee maker,
beside the sink, arriving without beginning,
each next to another without jumble,
each engaging small, very small,
grains of sugar. Each ant smaller
than the smallest corner of my smallest finger.
Grains are disappearing, microscopic
jaws are swallowing, minute amounts
of stomach acid are absorbing. Cells. Cells.
Another universe and within that universe
swirls and nucleic chains absorbing
without effort, without interference—
conscious/unconscious energy,
calm in its coding, free in its working,
cells-universe-connections-consciousness
ants-observer-sugar-realms

study twenty-six

and he saw light see
how it created the darkness
by leaving,
and something became something
that wasn't

and he saw that as far as he knew
he might be the first to see
the darkness how it
allowed the light
and something
became something that wasn't

and he saw that as soon as he knew
he might be the first or
possibly the second to see
how light woke within the dark,
as if it were flame within a rubbed stick,
he might free himself from sleep into sight
and something would become something
from something that was not

study twenty-seven

if you start seeing here's what you see,
you see the bird in the shadow under the bush,
he knows to be there because he doesn't speak,
so you may not see him, you see the stripe
on the chameleon's back when he jumps
from the fern to the branch, you see the need
to change in your own heart when age slows
the quickness of your hand, you see that
every and each vibrates and recedes
with every other, all sensing the place of all,
you see the going on and the crossing
from what was to what will be, as the frame
of seeing is reflected in the jacket you wear
and the hand you take, not for a moment
but across a moment, though you swear
as the bird chirps, you will not ever leave

study twenty-eight

alternating between actually warm and not
quite cold, winter left seams the crocuses
and yellow forsythia could move through,
wait! look! from beyond these windows
a pear tree bends toward the ground with its
exploding cloak of white, down in the elevator,
this head surrounded by countless blooms,
each bloom seeming the same from a distance,
each now a different size and part of
differently configured clusters—countless eyes
seeing from within, countless ears listening,
this is the moment consciousness no longer
resists its own seeking, *come,* it calls,
share this warmth, receive what I have stored
through long nights, built in the narrow
sun of short days, come, carriers of seed,
be here for me as I am for you, in the spaces
between these limbs I see higher limbs,
vibrant in deeper white, tall, darker trees
yet further up, themselves carrying green
buds still closed to the day, and further
the unlit windows of my rooms revealing
little of how I live, not even glimmerings
from the open book of odes where it releases
clusters of words turning like windows
toward this lavish speaking of Spring

study twenty-nine

it was an irreversible reverse
where the plate slid from the tray, struck
the ancient vase, the cerulean-blue
glaze falling through motionless space.
I could not stop watching. Longer.
Further. Lower. Perhaps it would not land.
I reached for it as it broke, hundreds
of pieces radiant across the terrace,
some falling further, falling through
the opening at the base of the wall, not
to be recovered among the numberless
rocks beneath. Numberless generations
had passed it from cabinet to tray
to table, each protecting the ocean-
deep of its blue, itself a message
from the chemical memory of time
about the nature of the heavens—*as
it is above, so it is beneath*. On,
went that evening's turning toward dark,
on, the slow resumption of the words
of the guests, on, the bird calls rising
through the fire-like eyes of the stars,
the glittering quiet of these eyes

study thirty

I used to hate her
now I love her,
bigger and biggest fire,
every tree in the neighborhood,
every voice on the block,
everything into the flames,
that was an extinction which sprouted flowers,
that was life with a femme fatale,
dinner with a fatal attraction,
dessert I couldn't slake.
I used to hate her
now I love her,
right down to the ground.
Are you awake? Wake up friend,
take water with your whiskey
and drink life straight,
the nights are longer
but the descents are from shore to shore.
Let this hair down, let it
all the way down,
let the mind let anger down,
and the graveyards where vanity
calls to itself,
and the many hundred weapons
and the established responses.
The Cossacks rode south
and those smart ones who were also
almost explorers
rode west and became partly Polish,
partly Belorussian,
and that was
the end of the Khan,
let the mind put hunger down,
I'm looking for one friend

study thirty-one

who was it who got up and walked away,
I was alone afterward, facing west
toward the west Los Angeles hills,
near to me a terracing of grey and green
scissor-shaped palm fronds, then a small,
or medium, valley's distance, then hills
where unseen breezes were pushing
fingers and hands of fog in among
pin oak and eucalyptus, then a further
hill holding up one umbrella pine,
a still point in the perspectival distance
signaling more and yet more distance,
visions of endless beginning where
the hills walk out and out and the fog
lies among them layering the receding
light, receding ridges, pine disappearing
into the last language of appearance,
the day into its shadowed holding

study thirty-two

when I turned in memory to the window
the five-year-old was sitting on a bench
five yards from her friend, who called
from her bench, immediately she pushes
herself forward, legs landing flexed,
turning, runs in split seconds straight
to her friend, takes her hand, leans her head
close, face intent like a newly opened
forest rose. What was there this morning
I did not hear when my sleeping friend
spoke to me? And what was there then
I did not understand when the Secretary
told me the plan would almost certainly
fail, thousands might be killed? For want
of a shoe a horse was lost, an earlier army
failed, *this moment finds itself in that*
moment, in a place I once was in, now
wake in these layered, generational cells,
to the clock of that returning print

study thirty-three

she appeared as guide out of the air
of a door which if it did not accept space
would not have admitted her, better
than I hoped and beyond what I thought
possible, she went out, she moved the door
where he was, when we returned, it was
clear what had happened—on two different
mornings she released his mind, on the first
he closed the door and would not look,
on the second he paused, he saw a boat,
an oarsman plying across a river to a place
where he saw he could be delivered
into a forest-like fullness of filtered light
layered with voices, without naming it
he understood it was a crossing over,
without seeking it, it was a resting place,
though no one there felt the need to say it

study thirty-four

landing in the uppermost leaves of the bush
his yellow-green chest moved moment
to moment from branch to branch, riding
weightlessly he was never not blending
in melodic consciousness harmony.
From there I turn toward the sea, rolling
beyond deep, bearing up green plants
and broad kelp, numberless shells, fish,
spineless echinoderms, all in buoyant
solution, rising, falling, aligning with
what they spawn. Tides washing over
sand, flies, life coming in, before the day's
arrival of not-breathing, not-eating, no
longer reacting, metal, plastics, glass,
the rejected half-lives of the manufactured,
the sea washing there, absorbing, bringing
down from the heavens the will to go on after

study thirty-five

at the edge of the hill which dips
down to the yacht basin I see a broad
bank of flowers, leave the tarred path
to go past that place of shimmering color,
look down — *there* — beneath the wet,
June-green stems of grass, *dark earth*,
announcing its depth, its immovable
presence, its everywhere present presence,
its sustainer of tree, flower, worm
presence, its base of birth, receiver
of death, presence. The present is earth,
all else holding to it, no other
everywhere sustaining, no single other
strong enough to be called earth, except
that light called sun which returns
and returns, staying sometimes long,
sometimes dark, behind a billowing
mass, here called cloud, and, yes, this
redder than red place of rugosa roses
which this spring, spring out of it

study thirty-six

this happened in what she used to call past time,
I got in my car and drove away, ten
minutes later and I would not now be speaking.
Here, take this car! I only want her,
as she was. She isn't as she was. I can't be
where I was not. I do always save photographs,
hoping the people will come back to fill them,
what that means is—I lost what I cared about most,
though I didn't know it at that moment,
haunting here, years dissolving through loss

study thirty-seven

through glass, mannequins in shadowed silence,
the many layers of time and distance part,
I see I had gone a long way from parents
as I began to believe in the limitless
reach of knowledge, individual imagination.
Not having had enough of holding,
raised in rooms charged with thought, thinking
one might live in every weather of the mind,
I see I only barely saw them. And after
the doors were closed and the cars had left,
they were gone, and what I had actually wanted
was to sit in any room we had lived in,
speak each word we had never said,
listen to them tell every truth and story
their parents had told them. Back through
the links of ancestral memory to what
could be renewed in these current days
and what could not. My grandparents there,
every mother, father, child, in connection,
more and further back until we might
understand what direction and what strength
had been lost. Now, as death begins its halting
whispers, and thought's hungers also weaken,
this becomes the moment I let myself go,
meet them on the shore of the never said

study thirty-eight

I wouldn't speak of this to someone
who wasn't interested in history—
like an empty sea on which a single boat has just
appeared, change can sometimes turn on one moment.
I left home when light was leaving the open doors
and windows of their house, everything flooded
past, those who raised me, those I knew in love,
those who reached across space and time with help,
those who tried to hurt me.
When I arrived further on
different hands were there lifting up some
of the same waters carrying the same warmth
and the same random splashings of scorn,
those latter I can sometimes laugh at as they
raise the questions, how do I absorb jealousy?
and who do I receive as friend? questions
for which I can find no answers, must leave
to the minds of the cure-it-all-for-you therapists,
here, in this place, I hold to the silence,
the calm, the towering evenness of air

study thirty-nine

beginning where we had never fully been,
the city seemed nearly impenetrable,
every store and building its own local wood,
each face a particular voice, each voice
spreading its wings like a wild, bright bird.
In the midst of economic crisis my newly-
joined friend does not stop texting, nor does
she stop looking into its windows for news
from around the corner. Is anyone here
who is waking here? Perhaps the woman-
mother who saw her autistic son unable
to voice his fear, lowered her head to kiss
his cheek, saw calm come to his face.
Every week a mud-slide of facts. Older,
and further on with each speaking at once,
it has become hard to hear the actual birds
in the occasional trees, which brings to mind
my father, his hair fallen through from black
to white as he spoke in my ear — *think clearly
about people and things around you*, which
further brings to mind the man who built a
Greek-revival house, while educating children
he had fathered with his elegant, indentured
slave, then paused to write The Declaration
of Independence, a text which remains central
to the variegated history of cities and freedom

study forty

power-driven water cleaned every corner,
even so he appears, darting in zigzag angles
across rows of tiles — from out of shadowed
gaps between the floor and the baseboard?
from unreached corners behind the oven?
Doubts, whispers, rustling shrouds surround,
still I hold to the larger certainty which
we take to ourselves when we decide to kill.
I fold the Times, leave shoes, tread, bend.
From years back, I know what I will see —
a hard, fractured outer shell, four legs
broken, two antennae, a disrupted network
of undersections, a logic in structure lasting
not for thousands of our sun cycles but for
millions, and not from here necessarily,
but from a place where this galaxy's energy
shifts and ghostly slides through another,
a place having been settled from beyond
its beyond, across unspoken distances,
by lives unspoken

study forty-one

I know nothing of the ways of clouds,
how they form, dissolve, pass rain
from their interior as we pass water.
Without moving they can be observed
to have moved, without speaking
they spread presence, sometimes soft,
sometimes like lightning. They don't
appear to drink or sleep, and why
should they, they are already in full
embrace day and night with the sky,
and, further, in one invisible moment
they have gone, disappeared, ascended

study forty-two

there out there are trees with their different
barks protecting them, there out there
are leaves absorbing sun, receiving rain,
staying awake and, indistinguishably,
sleeping in full chemical-energy-bond
with the open sky. No mothers, no fathers,
no ache of loss or wishing back the trust,
those trees are living in what we call
the natural harmony, this is still this time-
swept life, still this stone on this heart,
resting at a weight I alone can lift,
providing there is a roof, food, and,
indispensably, inspiration to imagine
the slope of a particular hill as the one
necessary dream, along and up the course
of which this wayward, tangled skein
called *us* might join, and linking, climb,
imagining a further hill, tall, with a yet
steeper, longer slope

study forty-three

how can we go on killing from a distance
and poisoning without sight each thing we eat
while it poisons us? To repeat—*what*
we poison ends in us. Will no one say no,
as our smallest cells say no, fly out
down the streams of the body, nerve
centers of the brain sending the message—
I'm sick, I am angry at your sickness, your
anger, which poisons with caged-chemical-
confinement each cow, pig, chicken,
every growing leaf thing—even apples,
almonds, fish of the sea, bees, you sleeping,
you lost continent of men, who do not
say no, in a country which does not say
no, which goes on stripping earth of seeds,
worms, pollinators, all sorts of carriers
and sustainers, in order to bend life
to the speech of machines, then turns,
turns formless, forgotten eyes to watch
late-night celebrities tell of their imagined
victories over the rebelling cells of cancer

study forty-four

we planted them when we moved in,
a group of two and a group of three—
a rhythm to the side of strong, rough-
barked cherries, whose blossoms wept
before the sky, then disappeared like rain
into the ground. Five lindens, each leaf
turning, turning back, absorbing light,
breathing wind, held by rain. Summer,
every tree, she says, *unhurried grows
itself.* And after four years, ten feet
of height. There, just then, symmetry,
a linked arc across the grass. Autumn,
leaves drying into brown, breaking
from the trees, scudding in the hedge,
nothing to hold them. Years on, they
are tall with broad reaches of limbs,
lost, the scale of our invention, lost,
her many-sided person. I find myself
lying on the ground underneath, seeking
to understand what it is they are
reaching for, their dark heads swaying
at dusk, almost blending into a sky
filling with darkness, her departed
voice saying, *there is only one world
of past-present, the trees are living in it*

III

study forty-five

more sad than death the thin evolving chords
for one left after, as if their life depended
upon each note being pulled through
the darkness of time's beginning,
from there, as if it were irreversible,
an expansion into light. I will continue
though you have gone before, I am nothing
special, except that I hear your voice beyond
the high pitch of here this silent listening

study forty-six

sunset, the Shelter Island Ferry landing,
burnt-orange light on the water,
the memory of my father's voice calling,
a small lift of sand and dune grass
and one silver olive tree holding light
like a sentinel, the woods beyond
already taken by the dark, the silver
olive trees of northern Italy coming
forward into memory, not I and not
anyone now arriving will live this again

study forty-seven

born here things run amok. People have
trouble. Voices you think you know
change. You didn't then fully know them.
You were the one who some of the time
seemed not to change, but not perhaps
to them. Passion runs amok on the rocks
of the bouldered beach—there's no life
alive without it. And still this brief,
small, waking into life—does anyone love
really any one? We speak the words—
is anyone here long enough to live them?
Youth returns in mind, it's not what
was lived by you, that youth was edited
by your own now not-remembered hand.
Parents return, but there are but few
of them, sometimes they do, yes, love you
in spite of you. Maybe you love them—
if they are actually who you believe
they said they were, standing over
the bed you believe you were young in

study forty-eight

sound fades from the passing train
nothing seems to change, I turn,
everything has changed, small increments,
corners by degrees, each moment replacing
the one next, succeeding waves of
beginning, the seeming and seeming again
of middle, the renewal and renewing of last,
which is the presence of this present, and
onward, the illusion of wealth, of more/less,
strength and more, property and less, fifty
years and five, all being replaced. I've walked
with each born from me, been gnawed on,
slept, walked on, held the place of father,
sung with each. What was produced passed,
is no longer, has been retired to what is now —
teeth and teeth used by the tongue for calling
one thought to another, while the layered
bricks of cities crumble, the words of
persuaders recede — the full place of myself
is this left after the sand of days

study forty-nine

this is what does go on, the road passing
through flat lands of brush and low trees,
the man driving, the woman holding the child
who cries then looks on with an untroubled smile.
More passes and more, silence between them
connecting to silence beyond them, afterward
a broad river where its several arms also
wind on in silence. The mother descends
into sleep, the child begins to seek attention,
the man gives her small hand his smallest
finger, her eyes slowly close, even
as she holds his finger. He sees the mother
holding the child, the child as she is held,
his heart is taken back to his beginning,
his mind to how long he has been alone.
It is night now, his head falls forward.
The mother wakes, speaks, a little further on
he brings the truck to a stop. Sunrise.
The child wakens. After food, the road.
Hills appear, the truck climbs. Bridges,
it crosses. The road broadens toward the city.
Many are going in the same direction,
cars turn off to the left, to the right,
when asked at the border who the child's
father is, the mother replies, *she has no father.*
This could be the road to Oaxaca,
to Bethlehem, to the American West,
each believes they are traveling toward
a lost world where they will be found

study fifty

mother and father parted under the same roof
and stayed, and within that ring of failure
a deeper feeling grew between them,
and what, and what else is there? There are
only the hands, the warmth I received,
the return I haltingly gave. I miss father
with the injured heart and the unconditional
continuing, mother speaks to me from
the measureless depth of night, I ask you
who are leaving—*take this message*—
they are always in my heart, I understand
what they did and what they held to as best
they could, I know the strength I left un-
answered and what I never thanked them for,
I know the years I cannot return to them

study fifty-one

is that the way it is, the mothers
want the handsome sons, the fathers
the beautiful daughters? Back and back,
generation into generation, human
holding, hormonal bonds. Sight. Scent.
Back and back, forward and forward,
continuous links within invisible chains,
arms within arms, each arm around ribs,
heart listening. Silent gravitation woven
through chemical code. Pulling, now
calling. Each speaking under the voice
of language. My guess as to how this is,
the layered print of the nucleic mist,
which here is me, there is you, mother,
son, father, daughter, never to be distant,
though children fall, become adults,
adults fall, become as first children

study fifty-two

the only way to find truth, my father
once said, is to seek for it yourself.
I could write my own history, but then
there would simply be my idea of others,
not the needs of others, their continuing
demands, all those eyes, words, my own,
saying this cannot be just history, this
must be knowledge of us, care for us,
a required painting-and-process-from-
life class in the school of Applied
Sciences. That's why I'm always asking
what it is I am actually doing and why
it is I am so continuously inquisitive,
like the flowers by the window which
I have sought to become in my range
of burnished colors. What flowers by
what window, you say. Curious, I say,
that you never stop speaking as if
you had possession of truth, personally
I'll try self-assurance some other time,
outside this inquiry, when I can forget
the multiplicity of things, the story
disappearing within this story

study fifty-three

what now is the sound of one hand clapping
or the sound of two hands clenched,
what now the silence of this mind,
where is the silence beneath the rolling of the sea
and where does the water wheel turn the silence within,
where does the silence within me
meet the silence when she shifts her scarf,
where also is the silence when the bell sounds
announcing this moment, it is and it is not here,
as it would be if I did or did not speak,
had or did not have answers, which, wherever
I was/they were, I would ask questions of

study fifty-four

and that was myself then
and that was myself there
and that was myself in the city of buildings
and that was myself in the country of guns
and that was myself in the company of money.
And this was originally
a Sonnet Moderne modern sonnet
which suggested the picture of meeting you,
even the life of knowing you,
and that *was* you waking me out of the bank
of purchased desire and continuing purchases,
and that *is* you waking me out of the city
of over-building, as in — where will the water
come from, where will the waste go to —
and this now has gone on long for a sonnet,
and thus I end thus, in spite of all
and every, with your arm and my arm
falling out of days into the time of together

study fifty-five

clatter of dishes being placed
on top of each other, women's voices
rising, men's voices between, metal
striking wood, music entering, inside
the center of many sounds no one sound,
what time is it? Everything is before me,
deep, very deep red chrysanthemums,
some with their backs facing toward me,
small, white daisy heads mixed in, many
already losing strength, four unmarked
willow reed stems standing. Age. Youth.
Space framing each. Onward into night.
Later night. Getting up, wanting to hold
everything in memory, study each thing
one more moment, study everything turned
on its side and in the near dark, *hold on,
hold on to time, let go now, now go*

study fifty-six

out of drek out of nothing,
out of merde out of no thing,
out of this resident refuse out of no one thing,
out of the place of the world out of has been
and is beyond,
none, none, fully known
none, not in part known,
none, none, unknowable
none, none, none, fully knowable,
beginning from there we are at beginning,
Monday cannot be the same as Tuesday
when counting,
and known/unknown rises
out of knowable/unknowable
when searching,
until the clock falls from the mantel
and chimes descend from the chimney

study fifty-seven

each thing tends toward dirt unless attended to,
settles lower, nestles, hunkers, digs down into it,
some things, of course, rise out of it, only to turn
and go back. I think of moles and worms, most
snakes, all of them moving in the manner of visitors
to an abandoned castle—up ramps and down,
spying everywhere, stopping to listen, remembering
their findings, pressing on to further rooms, there
we may be found, having raised a bed out of wood
in order not to obstruct their liftings up

study fifty-eight

each of us takes up things others
leave behind for us, she said, this may be
how this stream of words entered, still
passes through me, though it is beyond
my knowing where these words may fly
and into whose ears be received — by
a man whose own words I might receive?
by a woman whose knowledge, like a bed,
I might rest with? Clear now that I know
little of what my body tells me when
it signals there is food it will not eat, a face
it won't speak with, a history of myself
it alone possesses. Perhaps a journey to
a distant, unblemished beach would present
a more decipherable field, until someone
mentions what the oldest of us know —
there are no truths, only stories, some clear,
some hidden in a haze of fact, all needing
an unsettled sea to wash them ashore

study fifty-nine

missteps and pratfalls visit me,
friends and acquaintances mimic
from stage left, indeed what could be
more laughable than this weakening self
trying to hold to the fevers of youth.
Send more! Yes, the more I bounce off
the walls of this laughter the fuller I feel.
These eyes don't know when to speak
or what to tell, perhaps because they have
traveled with people seeking the answers
of finished understanding. Look, I can
walk, look, I can speak, and, as long
as I don't carry a gun, I can consider
how I began. Birth after struggle passes,
years pass, cover the house, become
what, failed desire? unmet hope? words
are succeeded by what? more words,
layers of would-be truth, think about
where they go, laugh, don't laugh, fall,
get up, laugh again, no regrets, no final
impediment, missteps bow to pratfalls

study sixty

how am I going to get out of here
and where am I going when I leave?
reality is most of the time an illusion
I nevertheless can't escape. Perhaps
I should move to the back, so it
will all be in front. I hear the small
steps of the mouse crossing in darkness,
believing it is safe, not remembering
there are others who will be turning on
lights, not remembering the smell
of cheese conceals a trap set in the dark.
Wake up to what you don't yet think,
the words that are rearranged so they
mislead, the army that invades far away
in order to gain power in this place,
ask more of yourself than you know,
wake to what you don't see

study sixty-one

ah, time, how many remarkable beginnings
you have shot through me—his small foot slips
onto my knee as he falls further asleep,
dreams of running through grass, his foot bending
the blades down, the stems not breaking.
The man on the opposite bench stands, walks
in heavy corduroy pants off the train,
the young woman next along lowers her book
of Tolstoi's essays onto her lap, pulls tattered
mittens onto her fingers as if she were
traveling across snow-bound Moscow in a time
before the energies of light and dark met
as photographic images on scrims of glass
we call iPhones. This is now the moment
his foot falls from my knee, this is when I am
alone, none left to connect to and no stored
photographs, though still sometimes in dream
you do come, lay your presence beside me

study sixty-two

immediately it rolls and tumbles out of the tap
spreading over the plates stacked in the sink,
reminding me of the sea washing over
the boardwalk and houses of the Jersey shore,
essence and substance that divides but doesn't
break, that driven against a small space can
lift anything. Think of it—lifting hundreds,
thousands of times your weight without effort,
think of it able to roll, break apart, re-join,
roll on, cover continents of deep land,
send evaporations to the deep sky, re-form,
fall back as rain into yourself, think of it
as if your children went out from you, grew,
changed, came back, went out again, came
back, no older, no weaker, still possessed of
every ability. Remarkable—yes? Grandly
flexible—yes? Can shed accumulations
of waste and also common earth, can return
to clarity on the moment, as if an angelic
presence had passed by heightening the color
of berries and leaves, paint, even coal
as it is washed. What might you name some-
thing which can fit every shape, wake any
color? The word water feels clean enough,
has some weight with its two syllables, but
misses perhaps the chime of the infinite which,
for instance, the French *l'eau* seems to hold.
Someone some day will form one of those
compound words, a seven or eight syllable
sound, imagining that each of its sounds
taken together might contain it, and perhaps
the linguists could dispute among themselves,

finally agree, until the older half of them
gave up trying to repeat each syllable, in,
what was that order? a complexity, they forgot
to remember, which could never contain
the roll and tumble of unbreakable water

study sixty-three

snow did not fall from the spring sky
though it was cold enough,
and I did not leave my entanglement
with the illusions of truth
though the tides of the world called with long fingers,
and yes it can be quiet here
if you are not stung by the sounds of those
cut by the lies of others,
and yes there are these beaches
where streams of light turn small fish silver
as they swim above the sand, and the continuous
rolling-in turns itself white
as the sand rises to swallow it, a closure
so effortless it seems as if it had been wished,
and if I look directly through this lens
there comes into focus a long departure of light
whose presence wakens
a sadness in the eye of continuing
which I now embrace
as if it were the end of my only day on earth

study sixty-four

where am I echoes from my eyes,
who am I looks down from the plain of ceiling,
what would I give to know?
here's what I see standing—
I am this room I turn to look out of,
I am the woman asleep behind me
and the man tending fruit in the street below,
I am where I put myself,
and where I find myself when I am alone,
I am the last thought my mind spoke.
Trees bend when the wind blows,
if it blows hard they let a limb go,
if you approach too close the crow
on the fence flies off, learn the lives
beside you, the many eyes, the bitterness
in their voices. I lean forward when words
are spoken, I walk to the front if the words
turn toward truth, if I don't engage,
the minds in front take the fresh words
out of the air for their own remembering.
I am where I put myself,
I am where I am when I am alone,
I am what I am when the mind expands,
I am what I am when I walk
and who I am when I sleep with whom I sleep,
wake the next morning, look into her face

Afterword

A voice was speaking from my twenties, *take off the title, step into an elemental language of things, the being here of things. No title. No capital as a mark of beginning, no period as a mark of ending. Open-ended examinations across multiple moments, through multiple perspectives. What might such pieces of writing be—not poems, exactly, but inquiries perhaps. Not quite, move further, language in the service of insight—a study.*

Earlier that morning when I stepped with shopping bags into my kitchen, began to imagine a theater showing a primal, shadowed heroine rising out of the shadowed bed of a silent film, there was a connection between event and my vision of something in addition I might think of not only as a poem but also as a study. Soon these moments of unexpected alignments began to expand, became sometimes meditations, sometimes archetypal maps, suggesting further movement. Studies would be open, transitional, able to reflect the mind's movements across space and time, between people, between lifetimes.

As the pieces grew in number, many began to relate interior landscapes using narrative lines. The Lakota Sioux phrase, *there are no truths, only stories,* came to memory—I used it in a piece then at hand. Some studies might have a narrative, others might examine something as substantial as earth, be connected to other pieces, nevertheless, by tone, texture of language, angle of perception. The question then arose as to what I mean by narrative. I am not suggesting what prose writers mean by story line — a movement from one point to another which, when achieved, has something of completion about it. Rather, I'm suggesting a search by the writer for events and images — I'll call them essences — whose selection may alter the reader's understanding. Journeys, I envisioned, not journeys ending.

As studies became a book, private conscience connected to public concerns. Issues of tyranny, justice, war, redemption, began to assert themselves. This would be a 21st-century inquiry, an existential inquiry, not solely an aesthetic discipline. The poetic field, as Auden, Spender and Thomas had suggested in the period between the two wars, should be open to *birth, death, sex, politics and religion* — subjects so central to living in this age of electronic connection and moral/economic dislocation, they have demanded to be included.

Notes

Horace is credited with inventing the Latin dramatic term *in medias res* in order to cast light on the means his Greek predecessors (Homer, Aeschylus et al.) had used to bring the reader into contact with the everyday back and forth of events.

study fourteen: everything goes into lock—trading activity stops, lack of confidence in the other parties' ability to complete payment

study fourteen: to own the code to close—trading in some artificial securities became so specialized that a particular electronic trading platform was required

study forty-nine: a portion of the plotline of the poem was suggested by the Argentine film, "Las Acacias"

study fifty-eight: *there are no truths, only stories*—a Lakota Sioux understanding

Afterword: *birth, death, sex, politics and religion*—a direct quote from Dylan Thomas in the early 1950s, when asked what subjects were appropriate for poetry

About the Author

William Kistler attended Stanford University, where he studied Literature and Philosophy. He was on the board of Poets and Writers from 1976 to 1992, and was president from 1980 to 1985. In 1983, he co-founded Poets House (New York) and served as treasurer until 2000. He is the author of four earlier volumes of poetry: *The Elizabeth Sequence* (1989), *America February* (1991), *Poems of the Known World* (1995), and *Notes Drawn from the River of Ecstasy* (1998). In 1992 he collected, co-edited, and wrote the lead essay for *Buying America Back*, a collection of 45 essays on America's social and economic issues. A strong supporter since his university days of a balanced, democratic society, human rights and environmental integrity, Kistler continues his commitment. He lives in New York, where he remains passionate about music and painting as well as poetry.

CPSIA information can be obtained
at www.ICGtesting.com
Printed in the USA
BVIC00n0130140114
341781BV00002BA/2